T0113780

# Strange Passion

## John Ngong Kum Ngong

Langaa Research & Publishing CIG
Mankon, Bamenda

*Publisher:*
Langaa RPCIG
*Langaa Research & Publishing Common Initiative Group*
P.O. Box 902 Mankon
Bamenda
North West Region
Cameroon
Langaagrp@gmail.com
www.langaa-rpcig.net


Distributed outside N. America by African Books Collective
orders@africanbookscollective.com
www.africanbookcollective.com


Distributed in N. America by Michigan State University Press
msupress@msu.edu
www.msupress.msu.edu


ISBN: 9956-578-85-1

DISCLAIMER
All views expressed in this publication are those of the author
and do not necessarily reflect the views of Langaa RPCIG.

# Table of Content

# INTRODUCTION

To most readers, the name Ngong Kum Ngong apparently makes its entrance into the Cameroonian literary landscape in 2006 with the publication of the poetry collection *Walls of Agony* and the play *Battle for Survival*. Such appearances, tending to suggest a writer's overnight acquisition of a mastery of the essentials of his art, and which have led many young writers into compositional pitfalls as they dash in frenzy for space in the writers' hall of fame, are often misleading. Thus, even though Ngong Kum – and one borrows a Gallicised metaphor here – erupted into our literary terrain in 2006 in a remarkable way, there was a pre-history to this, for his initiation into the long, lonely and arduous pilgrimage that literary creativity entails dates some three decades back. When by now he sings with a strong independent and authentic voice, this voice is a consequence of years of drudgery on compositional fundamentals that go back to his undergraduate years at the University of Yaounde, where the likes of Professor Fonlon held chair, and cultured, honed and initiated young minds into the literary art. This voice, now distinct, with certain unmistakable aesthetic traits, manifests itself, after *Chants Of A Lunatic*, 2007, here in *Strange Passions*, the third of his poetry collections.

Here then, as well as in the preceding collections, he writes with a compelling rhetoric force, with an incisive bluntness; revels in sardonic humour, and lines the lamentable, the impatient, and the defiant, that mark his tone with a sublimated sauciness, a verbal effrontery, called to the service of a resistance aesthetic and its noble socio-political ends. He pushes the two processes of subversion and appropriation of metropolitan languages that have come to mark most

*v*

post-colonial literature to great lengths, twisting, inverting the conventional structures of English and forging strange collocations to bear his thought and emphasise the engendering cultural milieu. When in 'Assassins' he curses that 'Someday their canoes will capsize,/ dunderheads who today like gods/ dish out death wrapped in decrees' or protests in 'Braving The Blade' that 'Venturing to dream dreams with teeth/ today when mambas roam the land is like braving a circumcision blade,' one instantly gets inklings of the hallmarks of his voice. Such defining traits equally imply a consistency in vision, in the ideological tenor of his work and consequently, when read from a synoptic perspective, *Walls of Agony*, *Chants Of A Lunatic* and *Strange Passions* reveal an overall evolutionary schema and unity in design, constituting a poetic trilogy.

In *Walls of Agony* the pervading theme is that of quest and hence many of the pieces there take the form of the invocatory ritual. It is the persona as humble quester, the ephebe as the Athenians of antiquity did call such, in his faltering first steps, on his way into the realm of art, humbling, emptying himself before Kezeh and Zekembi the divinities of his world, praying in 'Let Me In' and 'Before Zekembi' for divine hands to 'Mould me into a fine poet/ That my songs may my people revive [...] For a hammer and the word/ to crack the skull of terror' and in 'Invitation' in beginning of this pilgrimage which [is] 'urgent/ Very urgent and vital, soliciting power from Kezeh with which To dismantle the walls of agony / Erected in the heart of this country'. The hammer, crack, walls, terror, song, word, revival, the heart of the patrimony: the central images around which he weaves his compositions point to two moral preoccupations that will run through his work: iconoclasm, and from the ruins, rebuilding a new nation.

When we cross over into *Chants of A Lunatic*, Ngong Kum's hero has metamorphosed into Ntongwukuyeh, our inner voice, and the exteriorised manifestation of this: the priest-prophet, fully conscious of the burden of vision, of bearing the largely festering conscience of his people on his Atlantean shoulders. Here, in 'Upside Down Lives,' he treads Jeremiah's path, driven from society, 'like a castaway/ abandoned like a foetus/ [...] and forgotten at crossroads,' to howl from this wilderness about his compatriots' 'upside down lives/ dripping with pus of want.' For a society where moral sanity has been thrown to the winds, the obvious response to such obstinate obsession: nailing one's flesh on the cross and engaging in 'curing morbid conditions/ to cleanse the land of putrefaction' as he does in 'Medicinal Brandy', can only be what in 'Fall Not Prey' issues from the mouths of 'butchers of humanity/ spreading ruin across the nation,' and enters the possessed Ntongwukuyeh's ears as proclamations that 'I am mad.'

In *Strange Passions* his persona-narrator, the I with its possessive aspect, we, has evolved into a composite figure into whose moulding has entered attributes of three mythopoeic paradigms: the Greek Heracles (the Latin would corrupt this into Hercules) and Prometheus from the Olympian pantheon, and Ogun, audacious smith, warlord and pathfinder from the Yoruba Idanre Hill family of divinities. In whichever of these aspects we behold him in the poems, his vocation, his prime obsession remains constant – the soul of the nation. Passion, the central symbol in this selection, is thus to be seen as patriotic sentiments in their various manifestations: as vision pent up in the poet-prophet, now being discharged from his inner jailhouse of subservience in 'Bound,' through the medium of his poesy; as the undying, fiery patriotic zeal that in 'If I Cross Over,' 'will remain inflammable like petrol,' and which in 'Lucky People' does 'not fade,/ passions that make people tick/ and push them to duty, articulated in prosaic phraseology in 'My Weight has Fallen' as the desire to 'die loving you abused woman/ to infect the passions of patriotism and revamp the spirit of loyalty.'

As a Herculean figure he outlines his sanitising mission in 'Scrub with Vigour' as having to 'scrub with vigour beloved/ the fleshcreeping filthiness rats have/ painted the face of our history with,' and in 'Join the Crusade' as consisting in pushing his crusading knights to 'scrub immaculate/ the faeces of hatred off the bodies' of the nation wreckers who are 'battering the face of rectitude,/ crippling everyone on your way up/ galloping through faeces of hatred.'

After the benevolent rebel-god, Prometheus, who steals fire, thus knowledge, vision, from the heights of the Olympus to bring down to man, his persona is the visionary 'Drudging on the Esu hills/ your passionate piper [who] pines/ striving still your dreams to nourish' in 'Come Back Home;' an intellectual drudger, 'resolved to stitch our tattered history/ cushioned by the laps of forthrightness' in 'Fruits of Independence.' The ultimate end of all these endeavours as articulated in 'The People's Darling,' would be 'to clothe our vision with new garments.' But the poet knows that despite such rosy visions and what might appear as shrill optimism, the horizon of a new day does not simply slide into one's hands; that the road is one fraught with perils and agonies. He knows that striving to arrest my country's haemorrhage would certainly reap for him a Promethean recompense: outrage and slander that would in 'Taken Away at Dusk' ultimately lead him 'to the dark room of blighted hopes/ where they tortured to extinguish/ the obstinate flames of freedom/ blazing in his eyes.'

In the garb of Ogun the primal smith, intrepid warrior, artist and shield of infants, he in 'You Lied' sets out, 'thirsting for the ripeness of time/ to set flames on every crooked heart and set to music a new anthem;' to, in 'Strange' engage in 'running through/ hearts grown beefy on state sums/ and enjoy dragging them through unpolished terrain.,' In his crusade to shield the down-trodden from the ravenous drives of enthroned wolves, he will throw himself into 'neckbreaking tussles/ against those who dole out division/ than to down my tools to make advances/ for room in the bedroom of disgrace,' and in 'Killing Corpses With Love,' even move on 'to kill [them] with precision/ corpses with affection too.'

Ngong Kum's poetics is undisguisedly anchored on a resistance ideology, but where the socio-political commitment, this entails, has often worked against the aesthetic grip of many poets in post-colonial cultures as sheer propaganda comes to assume pre-eminence over art, he appears a self-conscious artist with an audacious technical dexterity that enables him sublimate the sauciness characteristic of his style and direct it towards ideological ends. Like the precursor of the English Romantics, William Blake, like our own Ogun's disciple, Soyinka, his poetry is as such marked by a certain noble fury and as a corollary to this, his rhythms many a time appear as the frenzied outbursts of the African masquerade, possessed, unleashed, in fits launching out to batter the occult cartels that have hijacked his people's transcendent march unto the folds of time. Seemingly thus possessed, he in, 'Join the Crusade,' can surge out in clamant chant to:

Crush the fleas flirting in your blood,

pound them in the mortar of spite
holding firm the pestle of fealty
to also grind betrayal of trust.

The vocation to art, poesy in such contexts becomes a corrective aesthetic enterprise: crafting subversive catechisms that would rescue the motherland from the fangs of mammonites on the pedestals of state power. Thus in *Strange Passions* as well as in the earlier collections, one cannot but remark the tone of urgency in the persona pushing a sclerotic body polity towards an apocalyptic lavation. In what appears like an initiation for a ritualistic orgy, he can thus in 'Killing Corpses With Love' sing of 'such strange passions/ that surge and pound/ like restless waves /against the walls /of my harrowed heart'; passions that will push him and his salvation army in 'Wooing the Sun' to 'breeze into campuses, / flush out pseudo academics/ and invite genuine intellectuals/ to commence sincere nation building.'

He appears to tread the path of Soyinka in our times, and down the line of history, Nietzsche and Sade, in his penchant to revel in a certain degree of verbal effrontery. In this, his poetic art assumes the form of a canvas in which the artist as wielder of images, as priest-doctor, delves for creative motifs, curative icons, into a magazine lined with the voluptuous, the pornographic, the canine, and the macabre for imagery intended to shock and bring back a cracked and blighted collective conscience to wholesomeness. His persona can thus in 'Bound' complain of his screaming verses that threaten him with '[...] the saucy sword of death/ hanging over those who slay art/ kneeling naked in public places'; and in 'No Wonder,' pummel anointed rogues in the pinnacles of power: 'Why a true-born father/ burst the drums of pubescents/ struggling the sun to lend them sufficient heat/ to roast reprobates like you?;' and in 'The Pain' capture the Promethean ordeal of poet-prophet in the stupefaction at 'the wrong I have done/ to be dragged in faeces/ like a dog without balls.'

Such a brief introduction can do no more than point to the drift of a writer's thought and the form he clothes this with. The full range and complexity of his style, the depth and density of his thought, the claims these could lay to originality or authenticity can only be sized by attentively going through his work. This notwithstanding in Strange Passions, one can humbly submit, Ngong Kum Ngong certainly makes a significant contribution to the relatively young cultural domain that is modern Cameroon Literature.

Kikefomo Mbulai<br>
August 2010.

# BOUND

I fear to begin these strains
infested with strange passions
but the muse, boiling with rage
threatens blowing off my head.
My mother, blind with affection
swears to die if I betray her.

The verses I want to write
are the ones the dainty nymph
dressed in sparkling silk, dislikes.
Blind with sentiments I bow
bound to pipe what she desires
or bear the brunt of barrenness.

I fear to begin these verses
screaming at me, drunk with fury
like bees attacked in the morning.
They want me to release them fast
from the jailhouse of subservience
strange passions, dancing in my blood
or face the saucy sword of death
hanging over those who slay art
kneeling naked in public places.

The songs the muse wallows in
are the ones my mother hates.
It is true dear reader that
blood is thicker than water
but I fear the curse of dryness.
My mother, grown larger in death
like a balloon filled to bursting

certainly groans beneath my betrayal
bound to explain my behaviour beyond.

## FORGIVE ME MOTHER

Chocolate mother
I know without doubt
I have let you down
turning my back on you
to cling to anything
I believe gives pleasure.
I know my strange passions
make you cry your eyes out
from the first blush of day
to the heart of the night.

I see you in my dreams
dressed like the setting sun.
I see you dark and bent
turning over the soil
looking for my navel.
You can't find it mother
no matter what you do
but don't be heartbroken
because I have let you down.
Forgive me lovely mother
even though my strange passions
make you bite your tongue daily.

I had to do something
mum, in order to live
on this side of the grave.
I had to do everything

to walk the earth without brakes
free to love what fathers rights
and accords bliss the liberty
to fly any time anywhere.
I know you are ashamed of me
and the commotion in your head
the machine of your hot temper
won't stop unless I change my tune.
All the world knows you nourished me
but I have my mission to fulfil.

## DON'T TAKE ME TO TASK

They drive me insane
wild choking passions
each time I see people
throwing stones at others.
They bare their bloody fangs
ranting and railing against
the melting mood in my eyes
each time I draw near people
 treading on the toes of others.
Whenever I try to strip bare
or stone to death these emotions
the heat in their veins increases,
pushing me to a very tight corner.

I tear drawing their wrath
or treating them with scorn.
I must channel their thoughts
 to avoid high blood pressure.
So do not throw things at me
when you catch me trousers down

throwing my shirt in the air
or sleeping with them in tears.
They make claims upon my head
ready to scratch out my name
from the book of versemongers.
The best way to disarm them
is to smoke their pipe of peace.
So don't take me to task mates
reading through these ugly verses
pregnant with strange savage passions.
Don't take me to task fellow countrymen
reading through these unpalatable strains
shedding passionate tears for silly souls
snoring while tigers devour their livestock.

## STRANGE

Some people love glucose
gleaned from the laps of pros,
others viands dipped in spice.
Some celebrate for life
the shipwreck of rivals.
Some weep when others bleed
and some laugh when men cry.
For others it matters not
if the whole nation stands still.

I love running through hearts
grown beefy on state sums
and enjoy dragging them
through unpolished terrain.
They too should feel the cuts
I often have gone through lone

trekking inward despite threats
to show you the muck hidden
in the laughter of traitors.

Some people like grey grapes,
others wine mixed with snuff.
Some make deals with witches
to top their hearts with hate.
Some curse when others groan
and some frown when kids grow.
For others it matters not
if everyone has dysentery
and reptiles worm their way
into the heart of loyalty.

You sleep with body-snatchers
the key to your breakneck rise
and cherish hell broken loose
as fire adores dry leaves.
'Tis strange that music bores you
and incenses your strange spirit.
Truth unvarnished I understand
upsets your massive stomach too.
The adder in your discourses
and the villainy in your eyes
put to flight myriads of brains.
Iconoclast, no smile of mine,
no shoot, no descendant of mine
will betray the battle I fight
for sanity to ascend the throne.

# NO WONDER

Just as night follows day
I know you will explode
and stampede like a bull
given your dull nature.
The oil of palmgreasing
and the perfume of self
running down your goatee
like pus from an abscess
make it hard for your heart
to feel the fervour of passion.
No wonder you stick to stuffing
credulous fools with fresh banknotes
stolen from the people's strongroom
instead of embracing the flag
for Cameroon to earn a name.

For sure you will fume
and curse like a whore
sick with disappointment
given your low mental age.
Your heart warms to no counsel
 and the flames of wild hatred
burning in your bloodshot eyes
 like dry season bush fires
deflate the drive to be one.
Why should the angel in you
moulded to bail people out
rejoice when on dung they feast?
Why a true-born father
burst the drums of pubescents
struggling to seduce the sun

to lend them sufficient heat
to roast reprobates like you?
No wonder you love running down
those whose passion for this nation
is a stumbling block to your resolve
to transform the country into trash
for your circus kingdom to take root.

## KILLING CORPSES WITH LOVE

I am flesh and blood
from the dust like you
but born on the breadline
in the backbone of drouth
near a dingle of skulls
far from solace and bliss.

The weathering weather,
the cutting edge of life
and the wolf at my door
have given me the nerves
not only to twine round
everything with a passion
overriding and straitfaced,
but to kill with precision
corpses with affection too.

I know you will
steer clear of me
let alone stand
such strange passions
that surge and pound
like restless waves

against the walls
of my harrowed heart.
I am conscious that
you will set your face
against my cri de cœur
to kill corpses with love
in this beautiful country
dying for a decent drink.

## CRI DE COEUR

O that you were highbrow
to scan your facelessness
or take into account
the fever in my bones,
the fire in my brain
and the eagerness to embrace
everything that brings fulfilment.

O that you were human
to sniff the stench of life
and feel the waves of want
hurling stones at me daily,
you will reach the reason why
I have chosen to fondle
even the breasts of corpses.

I have done everything
to offer you my heart
replete with pietistic love
to gloat over this life brief,
bursting at the seams like yeast
not on the milk of the land

but on the sweat of my brow.
I know my revolting lines,
my strange overripe passions
and my love for everything
make you sick to your stomach.
I know the shoddy entente
hatched in the parlour of sloth
when ignorance licked your eyes
and greed drove you into cash
frighten you out of your wits.

O that you were singlehearted
to feel the lack of acceptance
then you will hate passing over
the surname given you at birth.
You will do everything possible
to recapture lost territories
and reverberate my cri de coeur.

## THE PARADOX

I love everything that pierces
but abhor the thorns of roses.
The hot blood of fallen nature
tops me with vats of ecstasy
whenever I kiss anything foul.

I hate everything that assuages
but enjoy the caress of needles.
The affliction of the cowardly
fills my heart with refreshing waters
each time I urinate on efficiency.

I rest relaxed in thorny fields

and work distraught on cotton bags.
The fierceness of pregnant scorpions
overruns my senses dragging them
towards the sliminess of serpents.
The exquisiteness of ageing sharks
makes my ravenous inside rejoice.
What about you, strange compatriot
clipping the wings of celebrated truth
for an obscure theatre in politics?

## WOOING THE SUN

We woo the sun
each cloudless day
graduates in rags.
We hang round her
each flaming day
for flaming flames
to melt the iron rods of fate
smashing the skulls of gifted brains.

We will no longer roam
into woods without leaves
nor precious time waste searching
among the dead the reason why
our savaged hearts shouldn't riot.
We will breeze into campuses,
 flush out pseudo academics
and invite genuine intellectuals
to commence sincere nation building.

I will squat with them
these bookmen in shreds

in the east, singing hope
each day of my being.
I will sleep and awake
with them, the forgotten
wooing the sun with hymns
mortals won't understand.
I will turn to the stars
to give suck to courage.
I will entreat the sun
to dispatch flames of conquest
and call home those on exile.

## YOU LIED

Inayam, dear mum
I do not pour tears
in the bowl of time
for breaking your heart.
I weep because you lied
and sought to discard me
to mingle freely with pimps.

I do not sing your beauty
for laurels in dark places
nor your scruffiness expose
to be handcuffed and battered.
I sing because of your blindness
and because I pledged loving you
till the day death separates us.
I sing because my sly brothers
burning with towering passions
send to the stake without qualms
those who die to make you beautiful.

I weep and sing mother
to celebrate the storms
and the abortive attempts
to stand Reason before you.
The excessive heat of hate
and the frozen feet of love
threaten levelling us all.
Am dying to witness the day
Love and Xenophobia collide.
I thirst for the ripeness of time
to set on flames every crooked heart
and set to music a new anthem.

Inayam, my brunette
I weep to celebrate
the day you went astray.
I weep and sing, my love
to free myself from guilt.
You lied about my roots
to make the world love you.

## EYE ON GAME

I came round, Wiyam
my priceless woman
just when you stepped into
the room where I passed out
when I heard foul dogs had
ravished my blind mother.
You caressed my forehead
with kisses tender like green shoots.
Since then my heart beats so quickly

that without you standing with me
my passions run wild like phantoms.

Let not your heart be troubled
hanging on the skirts of love.
I will never embrace goats
though I cherish eating them.
I envy people whose beasts
unfettered by human strife
enjoy themselves without end.
They feed whenever they want
and go wherever they wish
not with conceited desire
but with an eye on big game.

I too need a reserve
into which I can run
for game for my kinsmen
whenever the need arises.
Moving corpses molest my move
weaving thorny caps for my crown.
I envy them not, the bastards
manacled to the wall of ruin.
I just want my crazy passions
 to race through your lethargic brains
and rend the cobwebs inside them.
So runs my metallic philosophy.


## SCRUB WITH VIGOUR

I want you beloved
to scrub with vigour

the walls of my heart.
Set down in public love
all the slime collected
and fall below my feet
for more room in my heart.

I want even maggots
to crawl freely near us
not men without livers
nor women with blunt teeth.
Let not my love for you dear
breed contempt for my passions
for my muscles can grow wild
and you may lose your eyeteeth.

Scrub with vigour my love
the room of our first love
where often we lay still
thinking of the best way
to thrust an arrow bright
into the belly of treason.
I want even crazy people
to settle down opposite us
not the green-eyed gory monster
wearing the mask of affection.
So scrub out with vigour beloved
the fleshcreeping filthiness rats have
painted the face of our history with.

# JOIN THE CRUSADE

Since I love everything spiny
forcing the mind to excavate,
demand not softbellied bully
why here I quarantine myself
slaughtering the lice in my head.
Demand not doubletongued ogre
why here in tears I make merry
like a young labouring woman
expecting her premier toddler.
Join the crusade to mop corpses
for this country to beam again.

Since I love what fires the heart
daring the mind to close combat,
I will breakfast and excrete pills
to purge your accommodating hearts,
you who kneedeep in the grip of graft
dress our wounds with bacillus instead.
I will send you clusters of thistles
to gore your drowsy consciences awake
and touch off the volcano inside you.
Join the crusade knocked about countrymen
that the cadavers we scour may shine.

Banish the banshees in your heart
bleeding the blood of belonging.
Slay the mosquitoes in your head
breeding blue funk and aloofness.
Crush the fleas flirting in your blood,
pound them in the mortar of spite
holding firm the pestle of fealty

to also grind betrayal of trust.
Bend your mind to duty freeloader
living on the genitals of vice.
Bend your mind to honour, dissembler
to dress Cameroon in new garments
today when raped morality mourns
the tomorrow of the human race.
Put your hand to the plough sycophant
to give birth to hope in hopelessness.
Join the cleansing crusade abused soul
and I will clasp you to my bosom
like mother duck her quaking ducklings.
Join the crusade entrapped backslider
for our fatherland to breathe again.


## FAECES OF HATRED

Overrun by remorse
my heart, cut down to size,
cries for the moon under
the eyes of intimidation.
The faeces of hatred thickens
but I will continue fluting loud
the keen flute of nationalism
thinking of passionate affection
dying to resuscitate the dying.
I will continue stroking passion
thinking of those not yet begotten,
those whose tomorrow may never rise.

You who dote on obscurity
and run everyday like a hare

16

after backbencher positions
battering the face of rectitude,
crippling everyone on your way up
galloping through faeces of hatred,
retain this of my ardent outbursts.
No nationalist dare stoop so low
to stitch the wounds of venality.
You who venerate lopsidedness
and run like mad after appointments
to fill your stomachs with anything,
retain this of my crablike passions.
They hunger to incise to the bone
the boils of callousness in your heart.
They wait ready to scrub immaculate
the faeces of hatred, off your bodies.
They wait ready to partner with you.
I see my heart breakdancing ecstatic,
floating above the ashes of hatred.


## A STAR HAS DEPARTED
(In memory of Christopher Okigbo)

Here in this once fertile orchard
now a jungle of ruthless minds
lies mother Idoto's high priest.
He fought for his people's freedom
but departed without notice
struggling to hedge his countrymen.
I have often caressed his mettle
bound to settle for bounden duty
that Cameroon may grow taller.

A black star has departed
yet terrorists play the fool.
A braveheart has passed away
like passing wind in darkness
yet blackmailers discomfit still
seeking to smash to smithereens
patriotism my battle ploughshare.
Okigbo's engagement twist one's arm
pulling my heart towards silenced poets.

A versemonger has crumbled
yet charlatans beat their drums
piercing the eyes of crabbed poetry.
Out of the bones of resistance
comes the incense of Watermaid,
fragrant in memory's plantain leaves,
inviting, solid like iroko,
beautiful and strong like a tigress.
I cannot resist such temptation.

I will homesick concertoes invoke
to smoke you out of your lethargy,
you whose affection for crookedness
has my homestead rendered desolate.
I will your wickedness lay open
and dump in the heart of the market
for carrion crows to urinate on
to tame the fever of my passions
and butter your way to liberty.

# DEEPS OF MEMORY

In the deeps of memory
innocent children I see
jumping in the Esu dust
their white laughter confounding
those whose passion for rape blossoms.
I see them still, the coffin children
whose tenderness and germfree passions
ridicule the wolves lurking in us.

Shall I ever again
play in the village dust
or doze in the Esu green grass
where often we clockbirds peppered
to kill our redhot hunger for meat?
Shall I ever again deathtraps set
delicious porcupines to entrap
to augment my mother's meagre meals?
Tell me lackadaisical brethren,
shall I son of guts ever again
caress the cuteness of my passions
to freeze the fear boiling inside me?
Shall I ever again my cradle pipe
beating virgin drums early in the morn?
Shall I ever again my mother's son
wake someday to admire her sweat blood
telling in song, happy as a cuckoo
the story of our provenance and fame?

# LUCKY PEOPLE

Peace delivered hermaphrodites
when she was thirteen and twenty
and at eighteen and thirty-one
but they too were androgynous.
The tail of her life was baffling
for she aborted seven times
and miscarried at twenty-two.

Her brother loved women at ten
when unable to play the cock.
He kept nourishing his instincts
until when he clocked seventy
and started ploughing a dame's farm.
Strangely she brought forth at sixty
geniuses with strange affections.

Such lucky people fear to die
but some love devastating wounds.
I am on fire with passion
for thieves who bring satisfaction
to a people clasping Death's knees.
Bizarre for an intellectual
isn't it folk, licking the dust?
 Some people moon after serpent tongues
while others fish for carnivore teeth
but I sorrow when biting shallow
and lucky people raise their glasses
to celebrate the death of decency.

I do not fear to die
since I learned to relish

passions that do not fade,
passions that make people tick
and push them towards duty.
I have sky-high-confidence
in people whose firm feelings
stir them to climb to power
on the ladder of free speech.
Such lucky people should never
fear to die when death gatecrashes
or democracy throws them up.


## DAYS DOWN SOUTH

Thinking of our days down south
and the sore sores we sustained
cutting through thornfields to survive
something intolerant breaks loose
inside my inside full of storm,
something determined to unfrock
those who maimed the experiences
we gathered trekking through rough terrain,
hoping we would someday feel at home
strolling and sleeping wherever we choose.

Thinking of those biting days
increases my cold sweat
as I watch in abeyance
the flames of unity die
and our children without hope
gathered round rotten apples
dying to covenant with dogs.
Thinking of those terrible days.

increases the bile in my heart
as I watch the coals of belonging
burn across the face of my mistress,
my country deep in tribalism.
Remembering those insipid days
when greedy masters gulped everything
gory musical notes sprout inside me
urging me to strangle tribal instincts.

Looking outside these days
through the window of time
I see underfed runtlike youths
groaning under the stone of fear.
Their groans like labouring wails
seduce the sanguinary notes
in the bowels of my strange passions
struggling to take root to go beserk.
Thinking of tomorrow makes me wince
imagining the wounds and the shame
history would leave on the faces
and bosoms of those without passions.
Thinking of the malaise that takes root
and the blood that often overflows
like a stream in the rainy season
when fey politicians come on stage
I weep over our lost identity
and wish I could Cameroon recreate.

# THE PAIN

I know neither my state
nor the wrong I have done
to be dragged in faeces
like a dog without balls.

The pain of being kicked about
like a football without lungs hurts
yet snakes in the grass make merry
throwing up through their posteriors
on the coarse carpet of falsehood.

Keen rage suffocates, reason tames
yet the passion to right rages
like a caged lion fired by hunger.
The fear of capsizing mesmerises
yet the zeal to identify burns still
like a bonfire in the harmattan.

Scallywags monitor my dreams,
not for my passionate verses
but for bitterleafed calumny
cooked in the belly of malice
to sacrifice on the altar of greed
my unbendable grief for Cameroon.

The heartache of an underdog
unearths the suffocating sores
contracted down south defending
mixed marriages at pistol point.
The pain of being made sport of
breeds bad blood and retaliation

inflating my bizarre piping
with triggerhappy emotions.
Tell me why I should not satisfy
the itching palm of cutting a figure.


## PROVOCATION

Another passion has been hatched
dragging me to the yard of skulls
where many committed mates sleep.
Frustration in multicoloured shreds
parades the streets looking for comfort.
The bronze statue of love we sculpted
has collapsed disfigured by neglect.
The union we forged in mortal fear
is bleeding to death savaged by greed.
Those who championed unification sigh
unable to bluepencil their ditched thrust
or raise a hand against one sidedness.

Now drips the bitterness
and the hope we filtered
like pus from a chronic ulcer.
The thought of losing something dear
cuts through the mind like a cutlass
slashing the limbs of venomous weeds.

The parasites and rats we ignore
laugh to scorn our extravagant fear.
The death stench of abortion sickens
and the antics of those we voted
provoke even the lame to rebellion.

The blood of fallen compatriots weeps
and my ravished mother's withering breasts
draw tears from the eyes of nationalists.
The tattered pages of our noble birth,
the insolence pissed into our frontyard
and the limping love caressing your breast
provoke new passions to retaliation.


## IF I CROSS OVER

Yewayam, precious arm,
mother of my children,
I know you will flame up
when you learn this of me
but let no trickster mislead you
for my love for you is like steel.

I have combed the country
stumbling most of the time
in search of peace and justice.
My commitment to this land,
like a woman whose beauty bewitches
has driven me to obsession Wiyam,
making me groan in mosquito dungeons
my woman, like a castrated hegoat
yet my passion for you priceless prop
will remain inflammable like petrol.

Scorpion strokes like drills
have drilled my senses.
Countless eunuchs have my love cursed
chanting death songs behind my back

and mambas my testicles ground
to whitewash their voluptuousness.
To be harrowed thus suffocates
thinking of the hoax of history
and the demise of nationalists.
But I will war on even on crutches,
sacrificing alienated passions
to rid my woman of hanging judges.
I will fight till my breath passes away
to liberate you Yewayam, my fuel.
Even if I cross over my beloved
let no bastard lay claim to our minerals.


## MY WEIGHT HAS FALLEN

Living with wolves is tough,
too tough for tender minds,
too gruesome for chicken hearts
save Zekemenluw pumps them
with the wine of forgetfulness.
Only rats gloating over booty
and donkeys seeking feudal import
can withstand such canines called life.

My weight has fallen woman
like exchange rates in Wall Street
in this graveyard of passionate poets,
here where scorpions the last victims smoke
determined to hemlock all passions.
I have a skilled psycho-therapist
inspired to monitor my passions
and destroy the forest of anxiety

dragging me through decomposing feelings.

My weight has fallen woman
loving you thoughtful woman
the fire that rekindled my zeal
and killed the measles of impotence
 that mutilated our first children.
Yes, my weight has fallen defending you
against the tyranny of little minds
that blazed to ashes our coffee seedlings
and ordered our last children to kowtow
for pathogenic pieces of stone bread.
I will die loving you abused woman
to infect the passions of patriotism
and revamp the spirit of loyalty
secreting blood to kill with compassion
the invertebrate thirst for illumination
that eclipses the path to prosperity.


## TELL ME

Tell me kissing cousins,
tell me the reason why
you excrete in my eyes
and vomit in my brains,
I who can neither my crown
nor my screaming lame verses
raise above my fungus window
nor my woman's love consummate?

Show me obtuse brothers
the goats I have lifted

or the money swindled
that you handle me thus
like a soul with sticky fingers?
Why was I brought forth among you
if not to construct our nation
and concrete our frail unity?
Wherefore have you forsaken me thus
to fight alone, empty and wounded?

Tell me standoffish folk,
tell me why I should beg
like an orphan in my own country.
Tell me that my rebuffing passions
may prepare for neckbreaking tussles
against those who dole out division
than down my tools to make advances
for room in the bedroom of disgrace.

## WATCHING THE SUN DIE

Often I have pondered lone
watching the sun die daily,
asking myself why the hatred
and the self-conceit amidst us,
why the deadly manipulations
and the systematic destruction
of the desire to delight in
the charming contours of Cameroon.

I still remember
the day we shook hands
by the banks of the Mungo

promising peace for our kids,
the Foumban accord in our hearts.
I remember the oath we took
to defend the tea plantations
we opened after independence.
But the way you prey on me brother
makes me fear the voice of tomorrow
and the outcome of the agreement
we underwrote to love till doomsday.
Watching the sun of our marriage die
is like watching helpless, someone drown.

Watching the sun die daily
brings to mind the pestilence
and the nervepricking rumours
that spread rapidly like wildfire
consuming all sympathetic hearts.
I remember still the carnival,
the excited voices in the dark
and the raw oath across the Mungo
that fractured the ankles of reason,
dragging us into the worst blunder
history has ever placed on record.
I love the gaucherie and the jangling,
the search for armistice in divorce
and the no difference effervescence
incubating as I watch the sun die.

## INDOMITABLE

I have withstood them stout
the strokes of bestial tongues.
I have withstood them crawling

through dung and lashing laughter
to fend for my marked children.
The grief of losing cherished friends
gnaws deep into the veins of courage
forcing the mind retaliation to breed.

Politics has gouged your eyes out
belaying garlands round your neck,
teething deep into the heart of trust,
cracking the bones of gullible chaps.
Your passion for grandeur rusts the mind
like concentrated sulphuric acid.
Your folly ridicules my constancy
encouraging the mind rebellion to nurse.

I have withstood them all,
the kicks of your small mind.
I have withstood them laughing
through the court of your folly
to brew hope for the disabled.
The joy of dislodging bastards
digs deep into the belly of hope
urging honour to unsheathe his sword
to defend his territorial waters.

I will continue to defy them
politicians seeking feverishly
to gag me like a dog with rabies
to achieve their devilish designs.
I will keep screeching like a monkey
skipping from one tree to the other
in the intestines of the forest
looking for mature succulent fruits.
I have taken my stand against phonies

and will battle on indomitable.


## COME BACK HOME

I who taught you how to sing
and climb the Esu green hills
each time sadness sawed your heart,
I who your tormented mind soothed
rocking you round beauty's garden
each time scorpions invaded you,
here I am broken but not bones
breaking stones for my honesty.
I wolf grasshoppers everyday
sharing my malaise with the crowd
because I cotton onto your beauty.

Drudging on the Esu hills
your passionate piper pines
striving still your dreams to nourish
woman, with the sauce of allegiance.
You tried embracing public servants
to increase the salt in my gashes
hoping that my love would diminish
and eventually wither like grass.
Impostors tried breaking bread with you
to litter the terrain with bastards
but I could never and would never
ever bundle you out of my heart.

Come back home waterlily woman,
come back catalyst of my passions
that together my disfigured love

we can say no to the taenia solium
threatening to erect giant mansions
in the bowels of our territory.
Return my magnificent floodlit love
to water the flowers of my passion.
Come back home darling before darkness falls
here on these inspiring green Esu hills.
Many a morning I have meditated
seated on the hills, the grossness of man
so come back home ere disaster erupts.


## SETTLE DOWN WITH ME

The redness in your voice
and the love in your eyes
have gathered in the yard.
The edge of your tongue slashes
through the vicious heart of spite
like a knife taming obstinate yams.

Jackals grow fat on our sheep
and politicians reap fame
from the garden of our sweat.
Mad cows have broken the fence
we constructed round our farm
and trampled the millet we planted.

Let us settle down now
you and I my woman
in the belly of self
to emerge strong and united.
Let us squash the head of temper

the monster that ruptures oneness
and shaves the head of honesty.

Settle down with me love
lest I knock suicide's door.
Settle down with me dear
to clip the wings of jealousy
and char the fangs of suspicion
sunk deep into our guilty flesh
like daggers in corrupt stomachs.
Settle down with me tough woman
to douse in the bosom of rain
the odour of rotting bodies.


## TURNCOAT

I wanted us comrade
to blossom like lilies
leaping around like twins
and toiling like soldier ants
since you and I became one.
The transplanters of division
and the sculptors of bitterness
twisted the neck of your senses
and framed you into a traitor
to treat your own like excreta.

There are times my brother
when in the heart of night
your voice lances through me
tearing to bits my credentials
in the presence of crocodiles

for a meagre meal of millet.
I cherish what bears bitter fruit
and bear insults from fettered breasts
to maintain our mother's failing health
in a land where conscience hardly weeps.

I wanted us my noble breast
to climb the pear tree together
to harvest much for tomorrow
but you throttled my aspirations,
fractured the legs of my affection
 and auctioned our plantain plantation
just to dog sadistic scallywags
dying to flower in latent minds.
I am ashamed of your activities
turncoat in the service of assassins.


## MISCARRIAGE

They bullied us into marriage
clinking their glasses at sunset
our fathers confident like lice
for room in the palace of fame.
They cajoled us into union
wagging their tongues in ecstasy
our mothers certain as morrow
for space in the room of History.

Those who opposed the matrimony
died in mysterious circumstances.
Worms have invaded the partnership
though we have begotten ten children.
Only those licking divorce saucers

know how the pepper of miscarriage
and the onions of infatuation sting.
My woman and I are no exceptions
 watching armless our children miscarry.
The urge to rise and strangle Injustice
lessens with the coming of sharp nurses.

We bear no grudges
but we hold it true
my companion and I
that when hope becomes dry
human beings don't mind dying.
We cherish the wild pulsations
we felt before the miscarriage
and love hearts that conquer hunger.

## MY SUN SHALL RISE

No, bedbug brothers
I say no lapdogs
to your overtures.
I cannot strangle my mother
for position in parliament.
No, myopic brothers, I cannot
for room in the backyard of greatness.

To hell!
Pluck out my eyes
to soothe your whims.
Invoke your tingods
to sow groundnuts of disaster
in front of my modest abode.
Slice to pieces my itchy tongue

to quench the thirst of criminals
but remember, my sun shall rise
and my children I am convinced
shall decipher your wickedness
on the other side of the stream
and lead you to the guillotine.

No, misguided brothers
I say no, foul fellows
to your degrading call.
I cannot clean your mucus
for marriage with wisdom.
No, voluptuous brothers, I cannot
for epaulettes in the heart of vice.


## UNWELCOME GUESTS

When I think in the past tense
how white eagles picked our eyes
and black hawks devoured the chicks
Fortune hatched behind our house,
when I think and call to mind
the champagne killed in Foumban
goose pimples celebrate the mess.

The donkey pride of youth
and the beasts of silence
 are guests I hate entertaining.
They keep knocking indifferent
on memory's overcast door
to frustrate my determination
of trekking the path of endurance.

They keep undressing my intellect
to discourage me from divorcing.

How do I excrete dependence
the snake guest in my intestines
coating my country with mucus?
How do you remain indifferent
when history's genocidal punches
bring shame bundled in relief raiment?
When I think of yesterday's folly
and recall the teeth of deception
that sank ankledeep into our flesh
the desire to divorce grows taller.

## STROLLING DOWN MEMORY LANE

Strolling down memory lane
your plaintive outbursts I hear,
pulling their hair like lunatics
bent on fighting with their shadows.
I recall very clearly, black snakes
the medicine men you delegated
to hypnotise and blunt my senses
to cart away our meagre petroleum.
I remember very well, castrated dogs
the uncultivated henchmen you hired
to terrorise and terminate my household
to feed fat on the plantations of our sweat.

I ceased to feel hot resentment
against you intriguing monsters
the day my senses resurrected

and deserted the cinerarium.
Pension off the boxes from Paris
and cancel the order from London
to consolidate our sovereignty.
I hope to chance upon Justice someday
bearing on his back bouquets of flowers
for those who were falsely prosecuted,
those who sought to reconstruct Cameroon.
When that day finally arrives brothers
I hope we shall love together fondle
inside the bosom of our petroleum
far away from foreign conspiracy.


## CRIMSON MARKS

I see them still
though you are gone.
I see them beyond doubt
through the lens of fancy
the crimson marks on your breasts,
the claws of multicoloured hawks
fattened on the millet of our sweat.
I see them still, treacherous brothers
the death strokes caressing your manhood
and the termites surrounding your homes.
I see them still, the extinguishers
preparing our mines to dynamite.

I see them still
though you are dead.
I see them beyond question
through the window of passion

the gaping wounds on your foreheads,
the maiden stitches on your lips
and the blood filling the gutters.
I see them still, fragmented mates,
the deep incisions on your breasts
and the iron lashes in your eyes.
I see them still, the bloody traitors
fabricating coffins for our breed.
How does one deny Justice vengeance?
How can I restrain my emotions from
constantly pouring tears into your graves
where free from the world's prevarication
you now repose comfortable like kings?


## LOVE THORNS

Those who concocted our marriage
now command from glass mansions.
The tapeworms of subservience
and the ravishers of creative minds
battle for conception ground inside us
to reproduce locusts and chameleons.

Those who once rattled love drums
now in black markets hold sway
munching the livers of the poor.
Still I labour, dubious partner
 to stand reason in their front yard,
those who once whistled freedom songs.

The thorns of loving intensely
and the scars of incontinence

drive me crazy, heartless partner.
Alone I stagger down slippery slopes
my heart piping songs of betrayal.
Alone I stand contemplating woman,
seducing death to paddle me away
from this place of infatuated reason
to the other side regenerative,
where creativity the mind impregnates
and cute delivery rooms are constructed.
The thorns of loving you crazy partner
bring but humiliation to our household.


## I WILL NOT DESPAIR

When I think of our disease,
the falling disease of greed
and the cancer of envy
chewing the bones of beauty,
my brain whirls like a whirlwind
and my bile rises like mercury.
But I will not despair sneaky spouse.
Your companions may stand their vigil
in garments of assault chewing hemp,
their visages sooty like charcoal
I will not despair sneaky fellows.

When I think of distrust
the virus plaguing us
and the jiggers of rape
boring the heart of our soles,
my emotions foam at the mouth
choking, kicking in fury then silence.

Your masters can hire mercenaries
in the name of structural adjustment,
their demands piercing like knitting needles
I will not despair brainwashed compatriots.

Suspicion knocks at my door
fierce, bloody, mesmerizing,
then the monster Jealousy breaks in
bloodshot eyes, sentenced by alcohol
determined to subdue to extinction
the desire to stand by our people.
I will not despair chameleon comrades
and do not mind dying for Cameroon.
I will not despair dishonest partners
and do not mind slaving for my country.
I prefer eating my mother's porridge
to wealth washing corpses away from home.


## INTRIGUING

It beats my senses
and makes my head turn
as if much wine I have drunk.
My heart bleeds, my passions weep
watching my darling die slowly.
The temptation to dagger smiles
prepared to stand up to our parents.
Those who remember yesterday well
mourn the untimely death of our love.

I have seen many people quench,
visited the tombs of real poets

and emptied my eyes in their cells.
I have screamed in underground prisons
crawling to make my people visible
yet my gullible brothers laugh to scorn
my panting wish to see Cameroon shine.
They have fallen prey to office seekers
my intellectual philistine dream mates
today when unity we yearn for most
to quench the flames of unpatriotism
threatening to consume the paddyfields
we cultivated after our marriage.
It beats my senses yet revolution screams
drumming drums of unparalleled liberty.

It beats my senses
and makes my mind wheel
as if dope I have taken.
My soul sighs, my spirit moans
watching my ruffled emotions
fight like enraged pregnant mantis.
Those who remember yesterday well
mourn the emptiness of the present.
Yes, they mourn truly our hopelessness.


## THE CANKERWORM

Next door chunks of rotting flesh
the thought of tolerance chokes
The dream for freedom reassures
but the cankerworm of greed jeers.
My patience hangmen deck with flowers
plotting to sacrifice my dream world

to refuel their foreign bank accounts.

Bigots high and low
dressed like nightsoil men
resolved their foul bosses to soil
slash the tongues of savoir faire.
They have pressured into exile
poets whose passions animate me.
They have consistently deflowered
the flowers that flower my passions
to ride in blood-propelled limousines.

A thousand armed cockroaches
man the entrance to saneness
ready to lubricate their lips
with the oil of our stubbornness.
I will exterminate them all
stuffing their lungs with insecticide
to purify the oil in your heart.
I know you will deny belonging
to satisfy those who charter you
but forget not your umbilical cord
buried on the other side of the river.
Forget not the principles you stood for
before ill-bred neighbours humming ballads
pulled the wool over your defective eyes.
Forget not that the cankerworm of greed
feeds even on those who featherbed it.

# TAKEN AWAY AT DUSK

Scoundrels cornered the scholar
and took him away at dusk
dragging him through the back door
my doctor doubled in canvas
to the dark room of blighted hopes
where they tortured to extinguish
the obstinate flames of freedom
blazing in his unflinching eyes.

Bastards threw dust in his eyes
and took him away at nightfall
dragging him through slimy faeces
my mentor fettered like a dog
into silence and emptiness
to castrate and coffin his vision.
Nobody on this side of the grave
knows exactly where they interred him
and no one can locate his assets.

Feymen outfoxed the poet
to parade the main roads
barking like dogs with liver flukes
bent on infecting everyone.
I can neither be transported
nor contemplate fully the moon
without making my spouse convulse.
She loves loading me with questions
whenever I mention you, my idol.
Nobody struck with this country's beauty
knows accurately how they entombed him
but his spirit my verses still irrigates.

# THE FOUNTAIN IS DRY

Rats reduced my Love to bones
to make merry with sly drones.
They divided his white garments
and took to task my loud laments.
Before him arose a mountain,
behind stood his hope, our fountain.
Throughout life he dreamt freedom dreams
and stood up against weaving whims.

Termites feasted on his eyes
dancing round a pot of rice.
His tears drew no attention
nor did his groans contention.
Throughout life he swallowed clods
yet found no pleasure coining floods.
Black bugs deflated him to nought
and threatened those preventing rot.

My throat is parchy,
my kids' eyes starchy.
Our fountain woman is thirsty,
the rehearsing chamber dirty.
Scorpions train where we did sing
increasing in my blood their sting.
The fountain of inspiration is brown
but I reject every reason to drown.

# FRUITS OF INDEPENDENCE

The offspring of independence
grown tough on flotsam and jetsam.
Though detested like scavengers,
liberty drinks for distraught hearts
we brew dying to lose our hearts
to knights that can champion our cause.

Rosicrucians adopted us
and Islam pitied our status.
We spluttered phlegm on their faces,
turned our backs on their hypocrisy
resolved to stitch our tattered history.
cushioned by the laps of forthrightness.

Today the door of Shalom
we knock strawberries in hand,
tears of remorse and rootlessness,
tears of our lame visibility
streaming down our distorted faces.
Though abjectness the mind flabbergasts,
we die our passions to inoculate
against the tetanus of corruption.
We see life through rose-coloured spectacles
confident we would someday congregate
waving not only green red and yellow
but sucking the fruits of independence too.

# I HAVE A HEART

I drank them all, the concoctions
brewed in the kitchen of hardship,
hoping to wear yellow garments
for cushions face to face Justice.
I toiled with all my driving force
confident the harvest of my sweat
would arrest my country's haemorrhage.
but harvested outrage and slander.

I chewed every morsel of wit
baked in the oil of Experience
and daily drew from his fountain
for comfort not far from Lovehate.
I pleaded with all my passions
convinced the fruits of commitment
would stop their countless abortions
but you unwisely sent three hussies
with fireflies to make my mouth water
forgetting my heart still changes colour.

No matter how long you thunder
having a dig at my passions
remember I still have a heart
yes, even for hermaphrodites
for their desires string so well.
No matter how long you grumble
sharpening your rage on my chest
remember I too have a heart
yes, even for prostitution
for dogs have decency coffined.
Bear with me disappointed comrades

if my strange passions irritate you.
I too have a heart skilfully woven
to absorb our crazy world like supper
or throw it up like putrefying meat.

## DIGGING TOGETHER

Day in day out they labour
those who survive by their sweat
digging through infertile land
bleeding, gripping firm their hoes.
Love breakdances in their eyes
clutching an empty stomach.
Giant bloodthirsty dogs bark
tearing the heart of sympathy.

I drudge with you brothers
on this slippery landscape
from sunrise to sunset
to fall in action with you.
Fear quarrels with resolution
squeezing taut the neck of courage.
Impatience pulls a gun on patience
to quarter the heart of certainty.
I excavate with you dear kinsmen
digging through mine fields of wickedness
to assuage the thirst of my passions.

## THE PEOPLE'S DARLING

You are our hope daring soul
the right star to star us through
this darkness that suffocates.

You are the people's favourite,
the best of the freedom fighters
to lead us through this aridness.
Tenaciously to you we stick
like excited public lice on heat
expecting a breakthrough any time.

Seasons have appeared and vanished
changing garments like chameleons.
The plumtrees we spent years nursing
have matured and borne healthy fruits.
But the plums have been carted away
to feed those who cripple this nation.
Faithfully we look up to you still
expecting to discipline hunger
to clothe our vision with new garments.

Another season would soon flower
and the desire to celebrate mounts.
Remember you are the people's darling
the right character to carry us through
seasons pregnant with uncertainty.
Their expectations will soon congregate
excited in your ravishing parlour
expecting a very delicious meal
to continue supporting you to live.
Let not the bestiality of the heart
and the wickedness of your associates
dissolve the humanity in your soul.
Remember you are the people's darling
the proper helmsman to navigate us
through treacherous political waters.

# HAVE MERCY

Have mercy on us Muekebeh,
we who water your plantations
and like all good raising agents
raise your prominence to the skies.
Have mercy on us great landlord
we whose blood repaints your villas
and swells your foreign bank accounts.

Our limbs are broomsticks
our veins fibrous roots,
our sight glasses of charred images
some broken, some dangling in the air
but all facing where often we pant
planting and harvesting for you boss,
burning like a candle our manhood
to keep you always comfortable.

If you fire us Muekebeh,
our diabetic struggling household
will collapse like a pack of cards
and litter the place with corpses.
Have mercy on us magnanimous head,
we whose votes cushion you in parliament.
Have mercy on us muscled Muekebeh
lest the seeds planted yesterday shrivel.


# TEMPTATION

Shuttling at bottom gear
through yesterday's landscape

when you and I, lemon lady,
like dogs in the mating season
clung to each other despite odds
by the banks of stormless Mungo,
 I feel like throwing up my lungs.

A raging fire burns
in the heart of ennui
yet rats have assembled
to hatch a new programme.
Thievery scampers down the tarmac
pulling along sacks bulging with gold.
Am tempted to join the booming gang
to give my children good education.

I see horses galloping
their riders hysterical
all ready like soldier ants
to pounce upon their raiders.
I see magma in their eyes
and smell the dung of battle.
I see whited sepulchres
take cover like frightened dogs.
Charlatans simulate charisma
while goats take dates with mercenaries.
Am tempted to slip on their garments
to keep my children away from wolves.
Am tempted to betray my conscience
to rescue those enslaved by ignorance.

# THE SILENT KILLER

Sadness returns
the silent killer
mourning in white
the loss of sunk friends.
Their absence cuts through the heart
like a saw munching white wood
and my life remains a riddle
beating hollow the senses of reason.
Even my strange passions are crestfallen.

Your innocence mates
I spotlight abroad
perusing the love lyrics
we wrote, fallen associates
to celebrate the birth of our union.
The hand of treachery struck hard
and like rotten pears your heads fell.
Forged signatures crammed the pages
of a manifesto drawn up in haste
in the high court of manipulation.

Sadness returns
the subtle butcher
weeding in grey
the graves of resting mates.
Their absence overwhelms the mind
like locusts invading a farm
and my love remains an enigma
vomiting contempt into your eyes.
Even my strange passions elegize.

Sadness returns
the heart of wreckage
trimming in guilt
the toenails of flop.
Miscarriage destroys silver linings
and lethargy slaughters a nation.
The love for mammon grows everyday
dispatching thousands to the graveyard
like AIDS, the bugbear of Africa.
I fear the claws of this millennium
and the gamalin in your voices.


## DECENT GLUTTON

I hunger like a starved bitch
after the meals in raw eyes,
waiting for some fat wallet
to drive me into cloud nine.
The fire in my stomach
battles for room in my spirit
for a festival in the night.
All my children, I am afraid
are afraid to see me abort.

I strive to make my flesh bitter
to keep vultures away from me.
I burn to warm congealing hearts
and drain the phobia in their blood
remembering the lice and the ticks
swarming freely in their consciences.
I yearn to urinate on small minds

but gluttony often drags me away
feigning peace on the mount of bitterness.

I do not want dieters near me
for the heart of passion is raging
and the day of reckoning is near.
I will go in search of scholarship
in the prison wagon of my soul
to offer mettle to the mesmerised
and condensed milk to the emaciated.
Everybody knows you shake like jelly
whenever self-assertion is mentioned.

I thirst like a hunting dog
dying to drink fresh water
for strength and agility
to hunt for its lazy boss.
The hot sensation in my bowels
and the hunger tearing your muscles
clamour for quick as lightning action.
You can go ahead and thunder out
for the world to polish your appetite.
I can survive sucking my mother's breasts
for the world to really understand that
my heart can only find genuine respite
when you start eliminating the worms
that have settled in my mother's bosom.
I am a decent passionate glutton
dying to eat the heart of greediness
grown fat on the silence of wheyfaces.

# COME, DAY OF RECKONING

We were tailored to love
creeping through gates of wrath
for room in the hall of nations
We were bound to sleep together
nursing the wounds of yesterday,
pleading with time for fair treatment
and sturdy nerves woman, to militate
against the plunderers of our wedlock
and pool resources to preserve freedom.

We crawled into ourselves
and built inside selfhood
until prejudice smoked us out.
We lodged an official complaint
but no reply wandered this way.
We defecated on goodness
and decency threw to the dogs
for space in the court of evil.
We kissed the feet of tin gods
for room in the mansion of Truth
but rejection was our comfort.
We were fashioned woman, to love
waiting for the day of reckoning.

Come, day of reckoning,
come without determent.
Come like thunder and lightning
prepared new life to conceive
for those born to endless night.
Come with steam and ammunition
for room in the room of History.

Determined like guerrilla gurus
we wait tenacious and confident,
sniffing the air like unfettered dogs
waiting to tear off into action.
Come awaited day of reckoning,
come, for we all wait to coalesce
and rid our fatherland of structures
conceived in the womb of malevolence
to kill our passion for things that sting.
I die to clang lances with cliquishness
before the flower of my dream withers.